Into the Splashing

poems by

Deborah Darling

Finishing Line Press
Georgetown, Kentucky

Into the Splashing

ACKNOWLEDGMENTS

First and foremost I would like to thank God for the gifts of language
and creativity. I would also like to thank my husband, Craig, for his
encouragement and support. Finally, I am grateful to all my mentors,
Nancy Eimers, Richard Katrovas, Alen Hamza, Scott Bade, Denise Miller
and my nephew, Blake Wallin.

Publisher: Leah Huete de Maines
Editor: Christen Kincaid
Cover Art: Christopher Darling
Author Photo: Jordyn Dryden
Cover Design: Elizabeth Maines McCleavy

Order online: www.finishinglinepress.com
also available on amazon.com

Author inquiries and mail orders:
Finishing Line Press
PO Box 1626
Georgetown, Kentucky 40324
USA

Contents

For Christopher
whose compassion and creativity enriched the lives of
everyone he touched

For Drennan
the son Christopher loved in the womb

For everyone
who loves someone struggling with mental illness

"Truly terrible is the mystery of death."
"Requiem" by Nicholas Wolterstorff

At the Guana Tolomato Matanza Reserve

The beach is deserted
except for a few fishermen,
silver lines into silver water.
Shell seeking, I step
out of the arc of a hungry wave.
It recedes, leaves
a battered conch,
split coquinas, shards of auger.
Yet, buried in the debris,
        this moon shell,
surviving violence
to land at my feet,
whole, except for the hole
underneath.
Where is the life that sheltered
in this spiral cave,
careening on a crest?
Good things have been lost
        forever,
but if I put the shell
on my coffee table

it will look perfect.

The Tragedy
(a painting by Pablo Picasso)

At age 19 Picasso and his friend, Casagemas, moved to Paris
where they got entangled in a love triangle with Germaine
Pichot. Subsequently jilted, Casagemas committed suicide.
Picasso plunged into a lengthy depression, birthing his blue
period.

I.

They stand beside the sea,
bent, barefoot,
she, wrapped in a thin shawl,
he with arms crossed,
their heads bowed,
together, yet separate.
Beside them a child,
touching the man's thigh
with an alabaster hand.
Their garments are blue.
The sky is blue.
The sea is blue.

II.

In 1900 every painting is blue.
He creates what his gut sees,
after love and death
at 49 Rue Gabrielle—
one table, one washbasin,
two green chairs,
two chairs which are not green,
one bed with trimmings,
one corner seat which is not in the corner,
two easels, one oil lamp,
one heater, one Persian rug,

twelve blankets, an eiderdown,
glasses, bottles, paintbrushes,
*a screen newly arrived from a war zone.**

III.

After our son's funeral
his six brothers and sisters
drove to the Hough neighborhood
in the heart of Cleveland,
stood in a row beside his mural
on the wall of a halfway house,
arranged themselves in order,
oldest to youngest,
with a gaping hole.
We have not taken a photo since.
Everything is blue,
even the face of my grandson,
dimpled and grinning.

*On a postcard from Casagemas

Christopher, This Morning

On Wolf Lake, a gosling
dives and does not surface.
There are ancient Pike in those depths.
The mother thrashes
and honking shatters stillness.

This morning I press my feet
onto the cold wooden floor, pour coffee.
Pen poised above my journal, I wish for
the flow of old melodies. Yet, how
can I sing? All I hear is the goose,
her black neck straining as she cries out.

She will know other springs.
Instinct will absorb memory.
But I am sheltered in a season without renewal,
the lake lying solid as a silver coin.

Driving North

We drove north at dawn
through Wisconsin,
past Madison, the Dells,
Ho Chunk Casino,
Chippewa Falls,
stopped at the Leine Lodge
for a good beer.
Through Duluth and up the north shore
we drove in fog and rain.
We could not see Lake Superior.
When my husband answered the phone
his face went pale, contorted.
I knew.
Separate in our pain,
we stopped beside the road,
listened to answering machines.
No one picked up.
Service was spotty.
We drove to the hotel,
stood in the parking lot,
broke the news
to brothers and sisters,
severed hearts.
The oldest chanted
a monotone dirge,
I do not accept this.
I do not accept this.
Five more hours, we traveled
over fog twisted roads
into the Twin Cities,
into fierce embraces.
I lay all night in the fetal position
by an open window,
let the sound of the rain
cradle me
in its aching arms.

His Left Hand

One
He has not slept for days, says he saw the Grim Reaper in
shadow on the living room wall. I let him skip school to sleep.
And now he will not wake up. I get him into the car. His younger
brothers cower in the back seat. I drive up onto the sidewalk,
around a garbage truck, and keep screaming at him to stay awake.
They treat him like a criminal in the ER; *we have seen this all
before*. While brothers color in the corner of the room charcoal
courses through a tube in his nose, reaches the poisoned recesses
of his stomach.

Two
The phone just keeps ringing. Finally, a ragged voice answers,
ten hours away. I hang up and call campus security. On Monday
morning my son sits on a hospital bed in the county psyche
ward watching cartoons. There is a flash to disaster, the world
crumbling in a cloud of dust and bodies falling from the sky. He
and his father weave their way home on I 94 through a throng of
terrified drivers. It takes weeks for his hand to stop shaking so he
can draw. It takes months until his eyes become his own again.

Three
His sister comes into the bathroom. He is naked to the waist
and his back is covered with slash marks, his left hand bruised.
The rope and crampons are still on the roof of the Episcopal
Cathedral. A neighbor saw him dangling and called the police.
He has a misdemeanor now, trespassing. We promise him a red
Ferrari if he will check himself in. We stop at Munchie Mart on
the way to the hospital. He buys a bottle of wine and breaks the
neck off on the pavement. In the ER no one looks at us as metal
chairs crash against the wall. The short male nurse wrestles him
into a strait jacket.

Four
It is Christmas Day and he is home on a pass from the psych
ward. We beg the doctor for his release. His kind eyes water, "I
hope you don't regret this." We chase our son, terrified that he
will elude us. He has superhuman strength, leaps through our
front window to escape. Shards of glass explode into the frozen
air. He cradles a shredded left hand. It takes fifty stitches. The
female intern looks his age, remains unflustered, sewing. I am
asked to leave.

Five
I hold a thin book in my hands. People pass from one black and
white drawing to the next. They nod and smile. There is a keg of
beer and someone spinning records.

Six
His photograph appears on the big screen at Radio City Music
Hall, casual in a sweatshirt, smiling. Above him is a bright
gold flower on a red flag, emblem of the School of Visual Arts.
Twenty out of hundreds who yearned for this honor walk the
stage. He reaches out his hand to the school's founder.
I am crying.

Red Flyer

I pulled you, my small son,
down the steaming summer road
and as you peered over the wagon
my soul spilled upon the waiting world—
humid hum of peace,
Queen Anne's Lace,
oak leaves catching the late light.
In that August moment
I felt certain of my wealth.
Diapered, brown-bodied,
you laughed me out of reverie
having no such depth of thought.
All you knew was that your mother
pulled the wagon.

Arriving in Cleveland

The house on Euclid looks the same,
guarded by two stone Dalmatians,
haggled from an antique dealer.
A red maple, freshly planted,
displayed proudly on our last visit,
thrives in a corner of the back yard.
And there is the garage,
newly cleaned and painted,
housing the 2008 BMW.

Now we embrace his widow
with her guttural animal wail,
curled son kicking in her belly.
We had everything.

I sleep on the leather couch
next to the heirloom cradle
piled with baby clothes
kept carefully for thirty-six years.
Sleepless in the half-light
I fondle and fold them,
while the hands of the clock
he bought in Paris
register dawn.

Fish Hatchery

My granddaughters clutch fistfuls of fish food,
toss it into the mirror of the small pond,
gasp at the sudden swirl of fins,
pink and silver in the slant of afternoon light.
It is so clear we can see the sturgeons—
armored bodies, prehistoric,
six feet long, fifty years old.
They lie unmoving on the bottom,
burrowed into velvet silt.
I want to leap over the railing,
sink down to join them,
silent under the young fish
as they flip and splash on the surface.
Weighted down with water,
I cannot rise to leap for nourishment.
Above me the cloud dappled sky
ripples pewter and blue.
People stare at me and point,
their voices muffled by water weeds
under the flash of salmon.

Smiling One

No teeth, double chin, boxer's arms,
your demands are constant
and easily met—
food, dryness, sleep.
I hear the meaning
behind your nonsense noises.
You are telling me,
little grey blue eyes,
that I am your sustainer.
It is I who weaves
a place of peace for you—
in this blue sky, wind chimes,
winter dawn.
I will pay the price of placid days,
measured as the steady-winged
pace of Canada geese
across the brightening sky.
They know where they are going.
I will take you there.

Wedding Ring

Around his widow's graceful neck
rests a silver chain, a wedding ring.
It rides her heaving chest.
I think of his left hand,
his drawing hand, cold,
and am glad the ring lies on warm flesh.

In her swollen belly
a curled son kicks,
already fatherless.
That cold hand will never
sketch a boy's face
or toss him a ball.
It will not grab the thin waist
of his grieving lover
or move the tiller
as the boat skims Lake Eerie.
It will not high five his brother
at the Cavalier's game.
That hand cannot be warmed,
nor our hearts.
They lie like cold stones
in the tomb of our chests.

The Viewing

I hover beside the last sight of his flesh.
He smells like formaldehyde.
I cannot see his eyes,
eyes that saw what others missed,
corneas that now give another sight,
but I can't accept his death as redemption.
Some think there is a slight smirk on his face.
I do not agree.
He was afraid of death.
I always feared he would drown,
keeling over into Lake Eerie
in his small sailboat.
It is the most dangerous of the Great Lakes,
shallow, choppy, wind whoshing
like the air in and out,
his lover, lip to lip,
as she struggled to save him.
Now, his legs are covered
with a green plaid wool blanket,
a favorite for naps.
He wears the tie with whales,
a gift from his father, never worn.
On the casket she painted a blue whale,
acrylic on mahogany.
Nieces cluster, giggling,
in black chiffon dresses
under stone archways.
But I am out to sea,
swimming in a warm ocean
miles from shore.
Sea gulls careen, screaming.

Into the Splashing

I seldom cry.
The day of our son's funeral
I rose before daylight,
sat in the tiny kitchen nook.
Poems were my tears.
Later, my husband wept violently.
Guilt sat with me in the pew.

Beneath stone pillars, stained glass,
his father's words broke the hush
born of awe and disbelief.
I will always remember him
as the boy who loved to draw.

His therapist whispered,
Your son loved you very much.
Did she think we doubted that?
What did she know that we did not?
Afterwards, on a cruise to Alaska,
she sailed among hump-backed whales,
dropped the necklace he gave her
into the splashing with a prayer.

Dune Climbing

All lake and sky
and the back of my small son, climbing,
this last day of autumn.
He knows the way over the dune,
        scrambles,
reaches his walking stick to me.
        I struggle.
This body betrays me,
child by child.
We stand above the water
on the far side of the dune, shelter,
to eat bread and cheese and oranges.
Walking home through the amber forest,
we bet on who can find the brightest leaf.
He wins.

Two Plots in Lake View Cemetery, Cleveland Ohio
"Suicide is not a remedy." James A. Garfield

1831–1881

The President is boarding a train in D.C.
when a bullet lodges so deeply in his gut
that the doctors never find it.

Under sheltering oaks and weathered stone,
an angel sits, face streaked by grief.
A flight of stairs leads into the grand rotunda,
light splaying from high windows,
and the coffin, flag-draped,
a long way from the log cabin in rural Ohio.

1981–2018

The gravesite is a field of umbrellas.
Hundreds jostle for a glimpse of the casket,
perched on two boards over a gash in the earth.
Roses, children's drawings,
drop soundlessly onto polished wood.
Three men in work clothes come
to shatter silence with squeaky cranks.

When he was eight
his father took him to a mortuary.
The coffins terrified him.
Can you be in that box with me, Dad?
Today his father longs to jump
into that deep, muddy hole,
rip open brass hinges
and lie beside his son.

After I Lose My Son, I Remember My Niece's Stillborn Child

I can hear the stillness
    in the black and white photo
      of my niece holding Levi,
    the fold of the hospital blanket
      arranged over her naked
        arm, sheltering his imperceptible head.
His father hovers at her shoulder, whispering
    love words.
        They wait for him to cry.

When the scope touched her belly, she knew,
    heard no tha-thump, tha-thump, tha-thump,
      saw only his still form suspended
      in the coffin of her womb.

She begged him to be born
    so they would not scrape him from his nest.

She remembers folding tiny white cotton shirts,
    stacking them in a drawer, singing
      through skin and sinew.

They never knew him. Six months unseen.

Yet, I have this gift. *I knew my son,*
    in all his grit and glory.
      His artwork adorns my walls
      and his son giggles
    with a silly space between his two front teeth.

Levi had been dead in the womb for days, decomposed.
    They did not even see his face.

      Forgive the granite of my heart.
      I am broken now.

Arriving in Cleveland II

I don't want to turn into the driveway,
listen to the wheels of the van crunch up stone,
expect to see him come out the back door,
dog barking at his heels.

I don't want to walk into the living room,
see the leather couch, wooden Eames chair,
the self portrait of his mentor in the 70's,
hear the jazz he loved, wafting through the house.

I want to drive right past
to somewhere I don't feel like screaming,
My son! My son! My son!
I try to make pleasant conversation,
but finally give up.
There are no words to cheer,
for now sorrow is the sky,
joy the isolated hawk,
perched for only moments on a dead limb,
soaring on the draft of a cold March wind.

Hampton Inn, Caryville Tennessee

We have been here before,
shocked that a chain hotel
just off the I-75 exit
had this view of hills
folded one into another,
reflecting onto unbroken water
like breasts hanging over
a still silver chest.

I remember dinner, Japanese,
where we watched the Cavaliers
on a small antique TV.
In the morning we sat on the swings,
first light touching the hills.
He turned for a photograph,
thinning hair wind tossed.
I don't remember saying goodbye.

Today, hills muted
with late autumn leaves,
I want to lay flowers
on this sacred swing.

We have never been here before.

Symphony

This cell phone brings up random memories
and today it is you, son,
in a black and white sweater with a tie,
at the Cleveland symphony with your sister,
you, chewing gum and grinning.
The picture gives the illusion of life,
as you guffaw and shift in your seat.
It is you, alive.
Where do I take this?
I turn to your artwork on the wall—
The Cleveland Symphony Plays Respighi.
This image is a piece of you.
I decorated the room in its color scheme,
earth tones with a hint of dusty blue—
a tiger crouching beneath the violinist's chair,
black panther lurking beside the bass player,
the musicians with flowing arms
that seem to be in motion.
I climb into my recliner to commune with you—
your jokes, your creativity, your soft heart.
You are here.

January

I have not seen a star in months,
    only this unspeaking sky
    that presses down,
    squeezes life from us.
        One twilight a full moon rose.
        I worshipped her
        until she was devoured by clouds.

My only respite
is this hour of candlelight,
orchid blooming beside me
shouting—*there is life somewhere,*
the coffee, strong and hot,
my pen, a blank page.

I can't imagine July.
I can't even imagine March
when the wind clears the sky
to a cold, hard blue,
clouds chasing over the horizon,
naked limbs flailing.

    Yet, it is always June,
        dark month of endless light.
    I hear sirens,
    see him in the ambulance,
    paramedics working
    to bring a heartbeat.
    I see his screaming widow
    in the arms of her father.
    I see his brother,
    sitting stunned in the hospital
    beside the beautiful body.

        I don't know if clear skies would help.
        Maybe this thick grey quilt comforts.
        Maybe the sharp light of stars
            would hurt.

Only a Breath

*"You take away their breath
and they die and return to their dust.
You send forth your Spirit
and they are created."*
                    Psalm 104:29,30

Still sleeping, she is widowed,
                    weighted,
                              dreaming that a man lies beside her.
                    The cat keeps her warm,
          purring in the soft darkness.
                              She rises to yet another day of
waiting,
                    her elastic core stretched to its limit
and she prays for the son of her sorrow.

Shuffling into the kitchen,
                    she flips the switch on the teapot,
                              glances at ultrasound photos
                    taped to the refrigerator,
          puts her hand to her belly, feels
                              a heel thumping her ribs
                                        and she prays
for the son of her sorrow.

She imagines herself on her father's arm,
                              gliding through dune grass
to her lover's side, promising
          til death do us part.

                              Five years. Only a breath
                                        and she prays
for the son of her sorrow.

22

He Was; He Is

At dinner his name comes up
   easily,
      in trivial conversation
and I say,
   He was an artist.
      show them images on my phone.
But that past tense takes me to places
   I do not want to go—
      to the phone call,
         the scent of lilies,
      the waxy lips, the muddy grave.
One word
        sets me on a dangerous path
   flanked by lethal canyons.
I try to keep my balance,
      hold onto an invisible hand,
   his left hand,
        his drawing hand.

I hear his raucous chuckle,
      shoulders shaking,
   and in the light of that grin
I feel the grip of each mourner,
        I was special to him.
   How did he make every person
   feel the weight of his own worth?

I want to be like him.

Opening a box of Random Photographs
During the Pandemic

It is something to do on a strange day
       in a strange month.
Even the weather is odd.

This morning I walk around the cul-de-sac
in a fierce chilly wind.
The red-winged blackbirds sing ok-a-lee,
perched on dead cattails down on the creek
where geese land, arguing.
Daffodils bloom against a sunny wall.
Now it is hailing.
Tiny white pebbles bounce on the porch.
It is February in April.
Even the earth is surprised.

I am also surprised by pictures of the past.
You, in your polar bear sweater,
Christmas 1984, three years old,
electric white hair, skinny bow-legs,
missing your two front teeth.
(You fell from a swing onto your face.)
You, a young man, all sparkle and strength,
beside the Gunflint Lodge up north
at our family reunion, minus one,
the year your grandmother stood up
from the couch and her aorta burst
two weeks before your graduation.
You, 2001, drug bloated and scowling,
on the dock at Hanscom Lake,
after mania almost took you from us.
You, grinning in your bow tie,
watching your bride step through
dune grass on the arm of her father.

At 9:00 the sky is still luminous.
We are moving towards the Solstice.
The long days grow longer.
There is no frenetic activity
to numb grief as I hold
these old photographs
      and sip my rose-thorn tea.

A Poem for Christopher

How can the sky be this shade of hard blue,
flawless, infinite—
and you are gone?
How can the beech leaves rustle like waves
on a pebbled shore in the June wind—
and you are gone?
How do I put this familiar pen
to these parchment pages
revealing my heart—
and you are gone?

It feels sacrilegious
to find any pleasure at all
in this spinning world.
Yet, I know that if I asked
you would tell me
to embrace the sky, the breeze,
the waiting page.

So, my son,
this poem is for you.

5:35 AM

I am drinking your favorite tea
in a white china mug,
sporting a bicycle.
Out the window I see your bike
padlocked to the wrought iron fence.
We are loathe to touch it,
a shrine.
We won't wash your shirts
that smell like you,
or touch your office.
The whole house is a museum.

You are everywhere.
You are nowhere.

Come home, my son,
to the house you love,
to your tree-lined street,
to the bagel shop for an iced coffee,
to your forlorn dog,
to the wife you cherish,
to your unborn son,
to us.
Come home.

Deborah Darling has been writing poetry for over fifty years, sometimes scribbled on the back of a receipt while dinner burned and a toddler straddled her hip. Family life has provided much of her inspiration. After the birth of her first child the nurse asked, "Can I get you anything?" to which she replied, "a pen and paper, please". This happened six more times! Now, she and her husband, Craig, traverse the country to D.C., Philly, N.Y.C., Minneapolis, Chicago and St. Joseph, Michigan visiting their children and grandchildren. Residing in Kalamazoo, Michigan, has afforded Deborah the privilege of participating in the lively community of poets as well as workshop classes at Western Michigan University. Another perk of this location has been the proximity to the gorgeous eastern shore of Lake Michigan. There she taught her children to love its wild beauty, gathered imagery for her poetry and processed grief. After their third son, Christopher, took his own life in 2018 writing became an essential piece in her healing. She hopes that these poems will resonate not only with those who are survivors of suicide but with all readers who have experienced loss.

www.ingramcontent.com/pod-product-compliance
Lightning Source LLC
Chambersburg PA
CBHW022052080426
42734CB00009B/1313